My details

Name:

School:

Favourite places:

Favourite animals:

Before you begin writing ...

Posture

1. Sit up straight at your table.
2. Put your feet flat on the floor.
3. Keep your wrist straight and resting on the table.

Pen grip

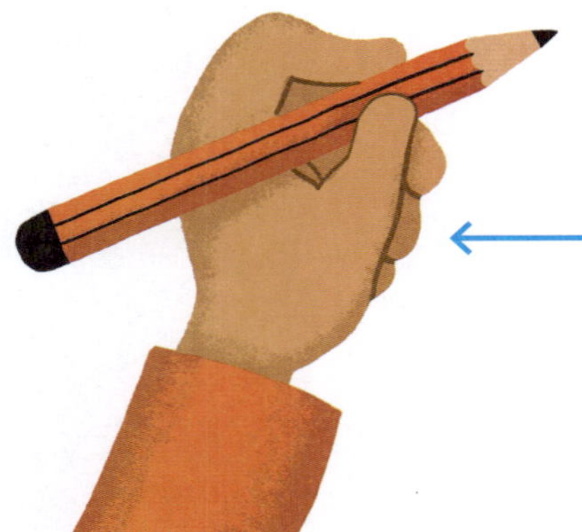

Left-handed

1. Rest the pen on your middle finger.
2. Pinch your index finger and thumb together gently.

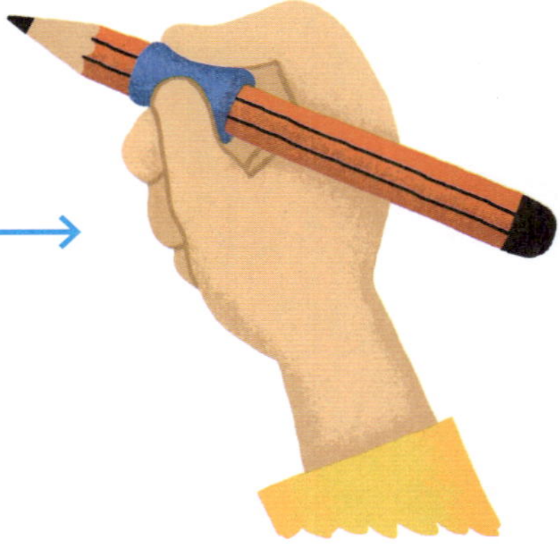

Right-handed

Paper

Left-handed

1. The paper is on an angle and held steady by your non-writing hand.
2. For right-handers, the page will tilt to the left.
3. For left-handers, the page will tilt to the right.

Right-handed

Revision

Letter formation

Before we start, let's revise the different types of handwriting. Remember that cursive handwriting is best for everyday writing and print handwriting is ideal for labelling maps and diagrams.

Copy these letters on the lines below. Then colour in the landscape.

A a B b C c D d E e F f G g H h I i

J j K k L l M m N n O o P p Q q R r

S s T t U u V v W w X x Y y Z z

In cursive handwriting, write your first and last name.

In cursive handwriting, write today's date.

Copy these punctuation marks on the line below:

. , “ ” ’ ? ! ; :

In your neatest handwriting, copy the sentence below.

Excellent handwriting is easy to read.

Diagonal joins

Before you begin, complete the checklist below.

- ☐ I have my feet flat on the floor.
- ☐ My back is up nice and straight.
- ☐ I can hold my pen accurately.
- ☐ I can angle my paper correctly and use my non-writing hand to steady the page.

Tip! Remember to make your diagonal joins go directly to the next letter.

diagonal join

in

Practise your diagonal joins as you copy the letters, words and sentences below.

le ne in am du de ur er hi ly un ci

uc he ty is ky mi ui ti te li an ce

sustain life planet living ecosystem connected

intricate world animals plants organisms physical

food components system supports wildlife biosphere

The Earth's ecosystems form an interconnected web of living organisms and their physical environments.

The physical environment includes both living organisms and non-living things, such as rocks, soil, minerals, water and sunlight.

Tip!

Diagonal joins exit from the baseline directly to the next letter.
After a diagonal join, the crossbar on the letter t goes above the join.
For a diagonal join to the letter o, go to the top of the o and retrace.
For a diagonal join to s, remember to use the modified s.

ut — crossbar goes above the diagonal join

co — retrace

is — modified s

Practise your joins to and from the letters o, s and t as you copy the letters and sentences below.

it ut to no mo ta as ts te ti ct co

The ecosystems include all of the different organisms on Earth and their interaction with the physical environment. This includes both living things (for example, plants and animals) and non-living things (for example, air, light and water), which are connected and interdependent.

What does it look like where this fish lives? Finish the scene by adding the fish's surroundings.

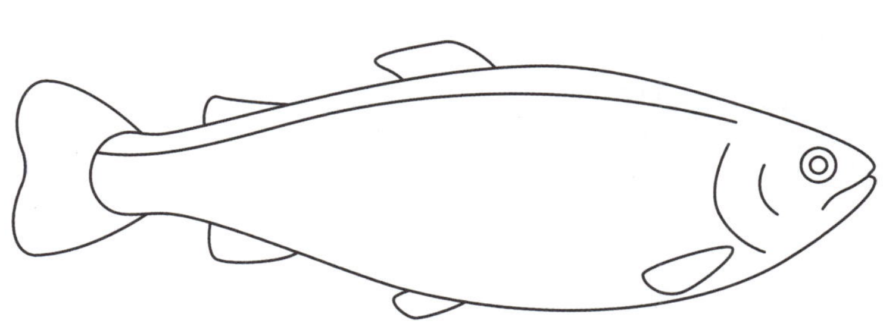

Drop-in joins

Learning intention: To practise drop-in joins

Tip! The letters a, c, d, f, g, o and q are dropped into place after a diagonal join.

I am successful when I can:

- ☐ sit with my back straight
- ☐ hold my pen correctly
- ☐ position my paper
- ☐ drop the letters a, c, d, f, g, o and q into place.

The dropped-in letter touches the join here.

Practise your drop-in joins as you copy the letters and words below.

ed ec ad ac eq ca id nd ma ic to do ta

land sustain habitat adaptation demand adapt

total population animals bacteria decomposer change

Copy the words below, which relate to the Earth's ecosystems.

biosphere ______________ communities ______________

biomes ______________ population ______________

biodiversity ______________ species ______________

Horizontal joins

Learning intention: To practise horizontal joins

I am successful when I can:

- ☐ sit with my back straight
- ☐ hold my pen correctly
- ☐ position my paper
- ☐ use horizontal joins from the letters o, r, v, w and x.

Practise your horizontal joins as you copy the letters, words and sentence below. For horizontal joins to anticlockwise letters or ascenders, retrace the top of the letter. Remember that joins from the letter r are optional.

on oq vi vo rg wa od va ok wo oo

of oa wr ol ro va oc ra ox ou wi

biomes without various warm survival wind

processes vigorous now organic own consumer cob

The Earth's ecosystems operate as a vibrant and interconnected web, where energy and nutrients flow through various trophic levels in food chains and food webs. Go online to read about trophic levels: https://qrs.ly/sugbcnp.

Self-assessment Underline your smoothest join. Circle a join that needs more practice.

Tip! Remember that top finishers (o, r, v and w) do not join to the letter e.

oe

Copy the letters, words and sentence below.

ro ve oc wa rc we od rg og oa

producer warmth forward variety destruction forest

Changes in one part of an ecosystem have ripple effects for the plants and animals living there.

Choose from the items below and write the correct meaning next to each word.

A problem that interrupts an event or activity

Involves using a lot of energy

The part of the Earth where there are living things

A substance that helps living things to grow

vigorous	
biosphere	
nutrient	
disruption	

Practise your joins by copying the sentences below.

A biome is a large ecological area that can be defined by its climate, temperature, geology and vegetation. Biomes have animals and plants that rely on each other. Examples of biomes include deserts, tropical rainforests, tundras, forests and grasslands. A biome can contain many ecosystems. Rainforests, for instance, have aquatic (water-based) ecosystems and terrestrial (land-based) ecosystems.

Colour in this drawing.

Peer feedback

Ask a partner to review your work and provide feedback on how well you completed your joins.

Two stars (two things you did well)

One wish (one suggestion on something you can improve)

Consolidating

Copy the passage below.

A habitat is an environment that is the natural home for living things, such as animals and plants, where they can find food, water and shelter. This is where living things interact with each other and the physical environment. Habitats are diverse and are shaped by climate and geography, which affect the reliability of resources. Examples of habitats are deserts, grasslands, forests, mountains, rivers, wetlands and coastal areas.

What kind of habitat is in your local area? Can you write three adjectives to describe where you live? For example, urban, rural or coastal, quiet or noisy, leafy or high-rise.

Teacher feedback

Practise your keyboarding skills by typing this passage.

Assessment: Diagonal, drop-in and horizontal joins

Sort these letter pairs into the correct join group.

on	ac	ed	aq	in	wn	eg	vi	ib
ka	ee	oo	ol	ca	ig	ng	un	ui
ea	wi	ni	un	uc	sa	an	wa	it

Diagonal joins: ______________________

Drop-in joins: ______________________

Horizontal joins: ______________________

Practise your cursive handwriting as you copy the words and sentence below.

regions carbon critical global ocean oxygen science

It is important to protect the Earth's ecosystems by using responsible and sustainable resource management practices that will safeguard them for future generations. One of the most important practices is using renewable resources, such as solar and wind energy.

Self-assessment Draw a star next to your neatest writing.

Practise your keyboarding skills by typing this passage.

Practising joins

Becoming a fluent writer

Learning intention:
To practise joins to make my writing smooth and fluent

Copy the letter pairs and words below.

pa se pe pr su bi br sa so se

people bloom preserve sustain soil blueprint protect

Practise your joins as you copy the sentences below.

It is important that people help preserve habitats to maintain the overall health of ecosystems. Even in urban areas, we can help by maintaining diverse gardens with local plants, protecting trees and looking after our rivers. Adopting sustainable practices can also help protect and preserve habitats by allowing plant and animal species to thrive. Sustainable practices include reusing and recycling materials, and walking or riding a bike to school.

Self-assessment Draw a star next to your smoothest writing.

Practise your keyboarding skills by typing this passage.

Word-building task

Practise your joins as you write the different forms of each word below. The first one is done for you.

Remember that we usually drop the e before adding a suffix.

Base verb	Suffix -ed	Suffix -ing	Noun
protect	protected	protecting	protection
adapt			
interact			
conserve			
interfere			
reduce			
preserve			

Fine motor skills task: Help Cooper through the jungle maze to find the toucan. Be careful not to touch the edges or lift your pen.

Joins to s

Learning intention:
To practise joins to s

Remember when you join to s diagonally to make the s shorter.

es si gs

At the start of a word, we use a regular s. We also do the same after a letter that doesn't join.

Tip! Use a regular s when joining to s horizontally.

os

Practise your joins to s as you copy the letters, words and sentences below.

os vs ts ws es is as vs rs ms ds

layers leaves oceans shapes across regions

A variety of biomes, such as tropical rainforests or deserts, exist around the world. Each has its own unique characteristics.

Fine motor skills task: Follow the steps to sketch the landscape, then colour it in.

Joins with double s

I am successful when I can:

- ☐ sit with my back straight
- ☐ hold my pen correctly
- ☐ position my paper
- ☐ practise writing double s.

Learning intention:
To make a double s with the first s the same as the second

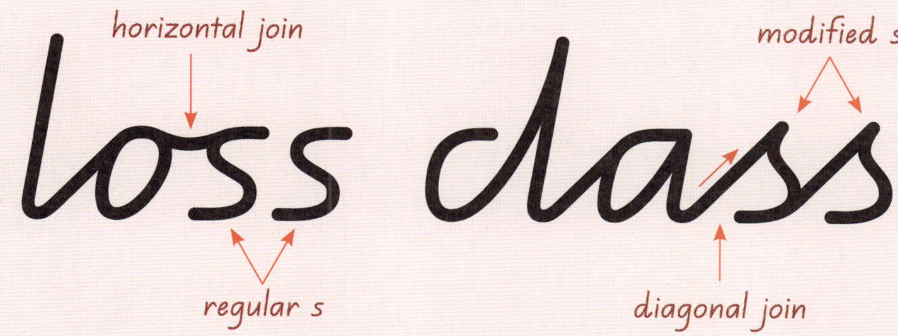

When joining double s, the shape of the second s should match the first. A regular double s is used after a horizontal join. A modified double s is used after a diagonal join.

Practise writing double s as you copy the words below. Notice that the double s looks different when there is a horizontal join before it.

mossy possible process across gloss toss blossom grass

bliss less asset necessary success discuss essential albatross

Practise writing double s as you copy the sentences below.

Successful wildlife habitats require careful management, ensuring that invasive flora and fauna (plants and animals) don't interfere with resources. Resources include shelter, food and water.

Self-assessment Draw a star next to your best joins to the letter s.

Practise your keyboarding skills by typing this passage.

Letters that do not join

Learning intention:
To make my writing faster and more fluent, focusing on letters that do not join: b, g, j, p, q, s, y and z

I am successful when I can:
- ☐ sit with my back straight
- ☐ hold my pen correctly
- ☐ position my paper
- ☐ write the letters b, g, j, p, q, s, y and z with fluency and speed.

Tip! Remember that s only joins onto another s after a diagonal join.

Copy the letters and words below. (Remember that the letters b, g, j, p, q, s, y and z do not join onto the next letter.)

ba ba be be bi bi bo bo bu bu br br

bright biome budget biosphere habitat

ga ga ge ge gi gi go go gr gr gu gu

green growth gorgeous large glacier global grass

germinate region garden geology gully geothermal

ja ja ja je je je ji ji ji jo jo jo ju ju ju

journey judging jubilant jungle jacaranda jabiru

pa pa pe pe pi pi po po pu pu pr pr

people place provide preserve protect

Practise writing letters that do not join as you copy the letter pairs, words and sentences below.

qu qu quest quality quiet question

source sphere safe support asset

ya ya ye ye yi yi yo yo yr yr yu yu

yacht yield youngest youth yearn skyrail yucca

ecology recycle organic juniper mangrove layers

Wildflowers thrive in grasslands throughout the world, adding colour and attracting pollinators. They include bluebells, wild bergamot and grevilleas.

Fine motor skills task: Follow the steps to sketch the flower, then colour it in.

The letter z

Learning intention:
To make my writing faster and more fluent, focusing on the letter z

Practise writing the letter z as you copy the words and sentences below. Remember that the letter z does not join onto the next letter.

az az az ez ez ez iz iz iz yz yz lz lz zz zz

breezy grazing zesty zebras zigzag blaze buzz hazy

Among the most distinctive animals on the African grasslands are black-and-white striped zebras. They enjoy grazing on the abundant vegetation. There are three different species of zebra: the plains zebra, Grevy's zebra and mountain zebra.

Fine motor skills task: Follow the steps to sketch the zebra.

OXFORD UNIVERSITY PRESS

More practice

Practise your joins as you copy the sentences below. Remember that some letters do not join.

Different habitats around the world, from the lush rainforests of the Amazon to the arid deserts across inland Australia, support a wide variety of species. All animals and plants adapt to their particular habitat so they can survive. Whether it is the icy Arctic tundra or the vibrancy of the Great Barrier Reef, these environments support life on our planet.

Rewrite these words using joins. Then colour in the rainforest.

vibrancy	______	supporting	______
survive	______	different	______
across	______	arid	______
species	______	life	______
variety	______	icy	______

Consolidating

Set a timer to see how long it takes you write this paragraph on the lines below. Add your time to the box below for your first try.

Grassland habitats are wide-open spaces containing grasses and smaller plants rather than large trees. There are grassland habitats on most continents, but they have different names. In Africa, they are called savannahs, whereas in North America they are called prairies. Grasslands are in the drier parts of a continent, usually between mountains and deserts.

Write the paragraph again on these lines, and note the time in the second box below.

Now type the passage on a computer. Add your time to the third box.

Time taken to copy text on lines the first time

Time taken to copy text on lines the second time

Time taken to type this text

Which way was quickest? Which version did you prefer? Discuss the benefits of both handwriting and of typing with a classmate.

Assessment: Practising joins

Practise your cursive handwriting and joins as you copy the words below.

scrublands plants between spaces people

supply grasslands sustainable parts blissful

understandable sparse typically burning seasons

Rewrite the printed script sentence in your best joined cursive handwriting on the lines below.

The diverse habitats of the world allow for animals and plants of many varieties to flourish.

Write your own sentence in cursive handwriting. Try to include one word with double s following a horizontal join and one word with double s following a diagonal join.

Teacher feedback

Fluency and speed

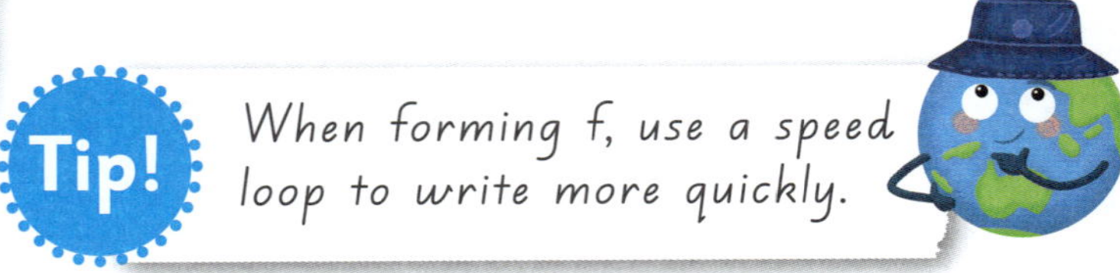

The letter f

no loop for the first f or after letters that don't join

loops for the middle and end of words

for coffee

Practise writing the letter f as you copy the words and sentences below.

found features flaunt reef colourful fauna

rainfall fish rainforest effect footprint diff

footprint offset tariff reforest surf bluff

Coral reefs are found in warm, shallow waters that are rich in biodiversity. They are home to coral colonies, colourful fish and other types of marine life. One of the most famous coral reefs is the Great Barrier Reef, on Australia's north-east coast. It is the largest coral-reef ecosystem in the world and was declared a World Heritage Area in 1981.

Practising cursive handwriting

Learning intention:
To practise my neatest cursive handwriting

I am successful when I can:

- ☐ sit with my back straight
- ☐ hold my pen correctly
- ☐ position my paper
- ☐ write in cursive with greater fluency and speed.

In cursive handwriting, copy these commonly confused words and their definitions.

affect (verb)	to produce a change in something
effect (noun)	a result of something
effect (verb) (quite rare)	to make something happen

Copy the sentences below, and then colour in the seascape.

Warmer ocean waters affect coral reefs, leading to coral bleaching.

The oil spill had an extremely adverse effect on marine life.

The minister tried to effect a change in environmental policy.

Practise your neatest writing as you copy the letters, words and sentences below.

ab eb ak lk ah oh al el ol ul sl cl ch sh wh

research zebu alpine waterfall brisk cobweb elk

peak brink altitudes alpaca elevation herbivores harsh

From snow-capped peaks to

alpine valleys, mountain

habitats are known for their

dramatic landscapes and unique features. These habitats

are characterised by their elevation and cold climate.

The above photo is of Aoraki (Mt Cook). At 3754 metres, it is

Aotearoa/New Zealand's highest mountain and a favourite

with mountain-climbers.

Practise your cursive handwriting as you copy the sentences below.

Snow leopards are elusive big cats that live in the mountainous regions of Central and South Asia. They have spotted coats that provide excellent camouflage in the rocky, snowy mountain ranges. Snow leopards have adapted to cold climates with their dense fur for insulation and large, furry paws that stop them from sinking into soft snow.

Use coloured pencils to colour in the different shapes in the snow leopard.

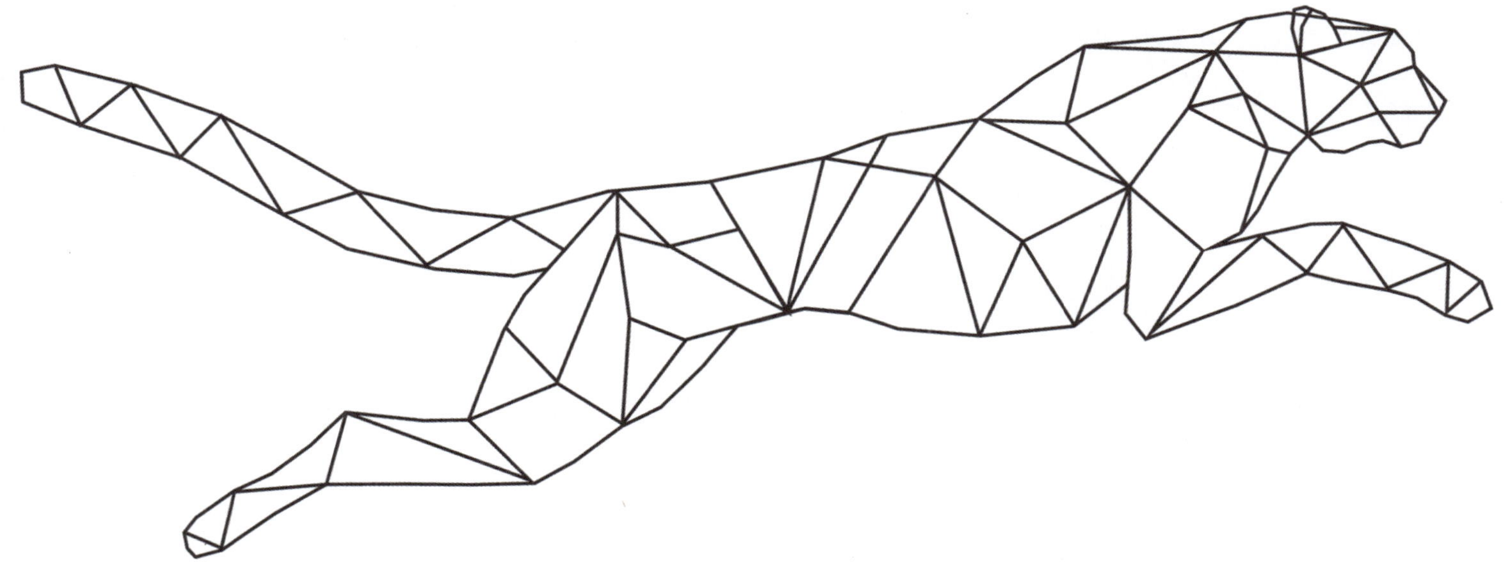

Self-assessment Circle the words with your best joins to the letter f.

Practise your keyboarding skills by typing this passage.

Practising fluency and speed

Learning intention: To practise fluency and speed

I am successful when I can:

- ☐ sit with my back straight
- ☐ hold my pen correctly
- ☐ position my paper
- ☐ improve my fluency and speed.

Tip! It is important to practise fluency in handwriting so that you can write in an easy and automatic way.

Copy these sentences. Try to increase your speed as you go.

Alpacas and llamas are native to the Andes Mountains of South America.

Sometimes confused with alpacas, llamas are larger, feistier and less woolly.

Llamas have an elongated face with large, expressive eyes and banana-shaped ears.

Write a sentence to say which animal is your favourite and why you like it.

Copy these words three times. Try to increase your speed in the second and third rows.

blossom branch berry

high higher highest

live lively lived

bubble kicker skate

Practise your speed as you copy the words below.

launch		landmarks	
traditions		harshly	
brook		natural	
creek		landform	
sturdy		skilled	
lagoon		livelihood	
breezily		hillside	
effortless		broken	
hollow		loosely	
wetland		horizon	
healthy		rainforest	

Consolidating

Practise your cursive handwriting as you copy the sentences below.

Tundra habitats are challenging environments shaped by extreme climates and are typically found near the Earth's polar regions. They are very cold places that experience long winters, with temperatures often below freezing. There are fewer species that live in this environment, compared to other ecosystems, due to the extreme conditions.

Peer feedback

Ask a partner to review your work and provide feedback on how well you completed your joins.

Two stars (two things you did well)

One wish (one suggestion on something you can improve)

Assessment: Fluency and speed

Practise your speed as you copy the poem below. This is the first verse of the poem. You can search for the whole poem online if you would like to read it.

"I wandered lonely as a cloud"

by William Wordsworth

I wandered lonely as a cloud
That floats on high o'er vales and hills,
When all at once I saw a crowd,
A host, of golden daffodils;
Beside the lake, beneath the trees,
Fluttering and dancing in the breeze.

Teacher feedback

Legibility

Printing

Tip! Print handwriting is often used for labels, maps and different types of forms.

Print each word neatly.

toucan polar bear kangaroo stingray scorpion

crocodile green sea turtle Arctic fox camel

cassowary lion horned lizard zebra panther

From the list above, write the name of one of the animals that lives in these habitats. Print neatly.

Arctic tundra	______	desert	______
grassland	______	coral reef	______
rainforest	______	wetland	______

Fine motor skills task: Follow the steps to sketch the bear, then colour it in.

Capital letters

Practise your capital letters as you print the names of the continents and oceans on the map.

South America

Antarctica

North America

Australia

Africa

Europe

Asia

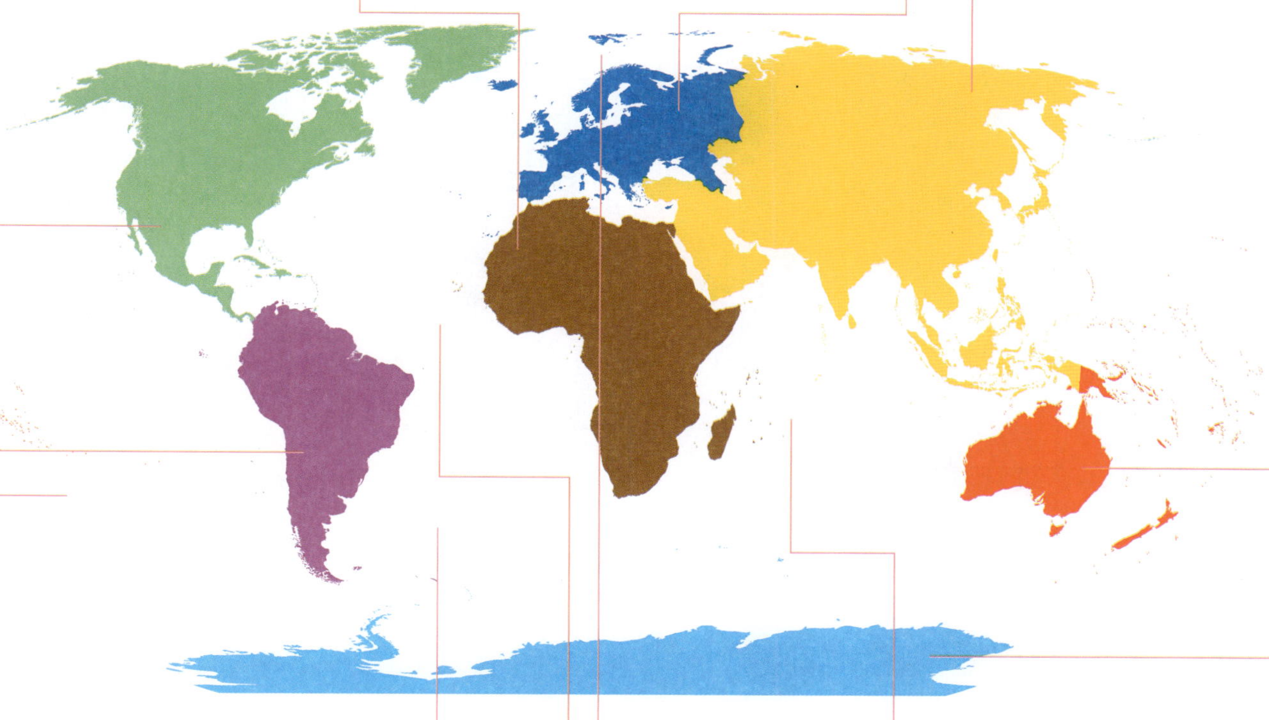

Southern Ocean

Indian Ocean

Atlantic Ocean

Arctic Ocean

Pacific Ocean

Practise your capital letters as you complete the crossword about animals.

Across

2 Rainforest animal that moves very slowly (5)

7 Dog-like carnivore of Africa and Asia (5)

8 One of Australia's deadliest reptiles (5, 5)

9 Wool comes from this animal (5)

11 Mammal with long neck (7)

13 Swings through the trees (6)

Down

1 Some are free range, and others live caged (8)

3 Biggest mammal on Earth (4, 5)

4 Black jungle cat (7)

5 Big cat with stripes (5)

6 Deadly desert arachnid (8)

8 Colourful insect (9)

10 Considered the king of the jungle (4)

12 Common farm animal (3)

If you need some hints, your teacher has the answers to the crossword in the Teacher Resource material on Oxford Owl.

Spacing

Why is it important to practise spacing in handwriting?

Spacing is important because it helps to make your writing easier to read. Even letter spacing makes your writing more legible.

Tick the sentence that is most evenly spaced.

Writing   that is   evenly spaced   is easier to read. ☐

Writing that is evenly spaced is easier to read. ☐

Writing that is evenly   spaced is easier to read. ☐

Copy the sentence below twice and try to develop an even spacing between letters.

Rainforests are some of the most intricate ecosystems on Earth.

Copy each sentence below twice. Then use a highlighter pen to highlight the line with the best word spacing.

Rainforests are lush habitats found in tropical regions near

the equator. They are characterised by lots of rainfall and

year-round warmth, creating excellent conditions for a wide

variety of plants and animals.

Size

tropical tropical

even letter size uneven letter size

Tip! Keeping your letters an even size is an important skill to master. It will help increase your fluency.

Practise consistent letter size and spacing as you copy the sentences below.

There are two types of rainforest: tropical and temperate. They have distinct features that make them unique to their location and climate. Temperate rainforests are cooler than tropical rainforests. A temperate rainforest in Australia is Barrington Tops National Park in New South Wales. Tropical rainforests are found closer to the equator and in countries across South and Central America, Africa and South-East Asia. A famous Australian tropical rainforest is the Daintree in Queensland.

Self-assessment Draw a star next to the line with the most consistent letter size.

Practise your keyboarding skills by typing this passage.

Slope

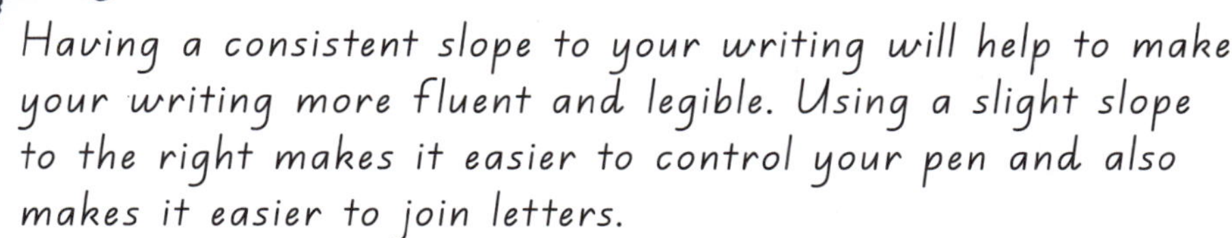

Tip! Having a consistent slope to your writing will help to make your writing more fluent and legible. Using a slight slope to the right makes it easier to control your pen and also makes it easier to join letters.

Write this word five times, using the slope lines as a guide.

equator

Circle the words with an inconsistent slope. Then, write all of the words using a consistent slope.

temperate warm emergent coasts

canopy dense rainfall climate

Practise a consistent slope as you copy the sentences below.

The hallmark of a rainforest is its towering trees, which form a multi-layered canopy. Tropical rainforests are home to numerous species of animals and plants. Although temperate rainforests have fewer plant and animal species, they are home to many birds, amphibians, insects, reptiles and large mammals.

Labelling

The layers of a tropical rainforest are shown below. Next to each heading, add dot points describing each layer. You may want to do some online research before you begin. The first one is done for you. Print neatly.

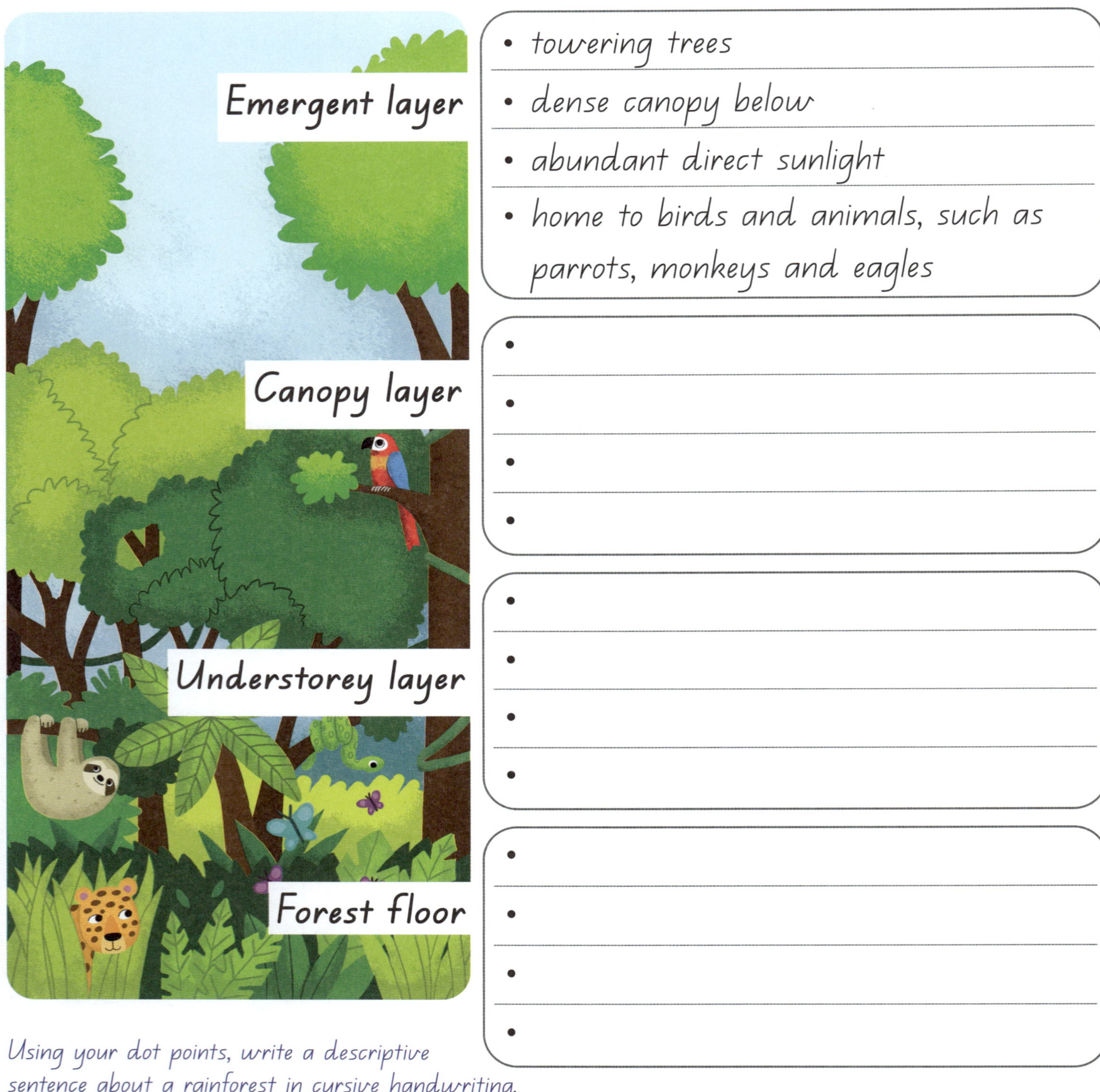

Emergent layer

- towering trees
- dense canopy below
- abundant direct sunlight
- home to birds and animals, such as parrots, monkeys and eagles

Canopy layer

-
-
-
-

Understorey layer

-
-
-
-

Forest floor

-
-
-
-

Using your dot points, write a descriptive sentence about a rainforest in cursive handwriting.

Practising size, slope and spacing

Learning intention:
To practise maintaining consistent size, slope and spacing in my handwriting

I am successful when I can:

- ☐ keep my letter size, slope and spacing even.

Focus on your letter size, slope and spacing as you copy the sentences below.

The towering trees of a

rainforest can reach staggering

heights. Emergent trees pierce

through the canopy to receive

maximum sunlight. The canopy

itself creates a dense and

shaded environment beneath it.

Fine motor skills task: Draw two of your favourite trees, then colour them in.

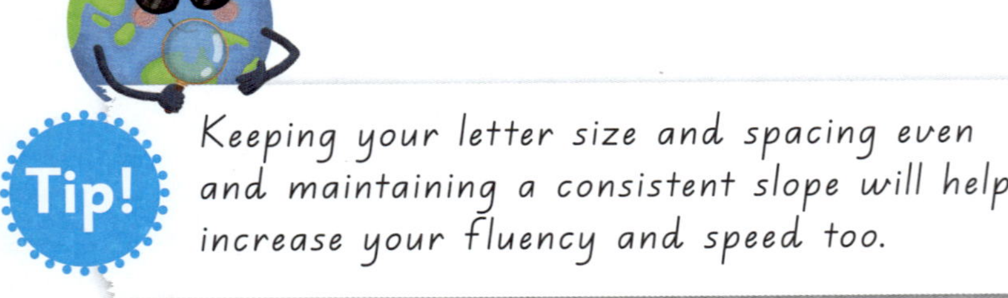

Practise your cursive handwriting as you copy the sentences below.

Rainforests are home to a multitude of animals and plants. Rainforests support a web of interconnected species, each playing a role in the balance and functioning of this intricate ecosystem. Some species that live in rainforests include monkeys, sloths, orangutans, gorillas, frogs and chameleons.

Finish the scene by adding the chameleon's surroundings in a rainforest. Then colour in the picture.

Fluency

These words are often misspelt. Practise your cursive handwriting as you copy them.

calendar fulfil separate maintenance quiet

beautiful experience receive privilege Arctic

achieve accommodate fascinating definitely foreign

Word-building task

In cursive handwriting, add the morphographs (word parts) together. The first one is done for you.

Remember to change the y to an i before adding the suffix. We usually drop the e before adding a suffix.

create + ive = creative

peace + ful + ly = ______

pro + port + ion = ______

un + ex + plain + ed = ______

re + late + ion = ______

noise + y + ness = ______

un + like + ly + ness = ______

re + cent + ly = ______

in + cure + able = ______

city + es = ______

room + y + ness = ______

The rainforest is home to some fascinating and unique birds. Practise your speed, fluency and cursive handwriting as you copy the sentences on this page and the next.

Cassowary

Cassowaries are large, flightless birds that are native to the rainforests of north-eastern Australia and New Guinea. They have striking blue facial skin and a helmet-like casque on their heads. The casque protects the cassowary as it moves through the forest. Cassowaries have three-toed feet with a sharp claw on the inner toe that helps them dig for food and ward off predators.

Scarlet macaw

An iconic bird that is native to the rainforests of Central and South America is the scarlet macaw. Known for its vibrant colours, it spends much of its time in the canopy. These beautiful, large parrots can measure up to 83 cm from beak to tail.

Toucan

Found in the rainforests of Central and South America, toucans have an unusual appearance. Their most distinctive feature is their large and colourful bill.

Copy this definition of an adverb.

An adverb is a word that modifies or describes a verb, adjective or another adverb.

Copy the sentence below. Then use a highlighter pen to highlight the adverbs.

Vividly coloured toucans soar gracefully through the dense rainforest canopy.

Copy these adverbs.

kindly carefully warmly safely

beautifully politely bravely gracefully

honestly vividly quickly always

certainly softly foolishly usually

In cursive handwriting, write about a bird of the rainforest and describe its behaviour. Include at least three adverbs and use complete sentences.

Consolidating

Practise your speed and fluency as you copy the sentences below.

Animals and plants have adapted to survive in their environment over many years. This has helped them to improve their chances of survival. An "adaptation" is a feature of a living thing that helps it adjust to its habitat. For example, chameleons are able to change colour. They do this to blend in with their surroundings, regulate their body temperature or attract a potential mate. Koalas have adapted to eat only eucalyptus leaves. This gives them an advantage because the leaves are toxic to most animals.

Fine motor skills task: Follow the steps to sketch the bird, then colour it in.

Practise your keyboarding skills by typing this passage.

Speed test

It is important to master fluent and speedy handwriting. Practising your speed in forming letters and words can help to improve overall proficiency.

Read the sentence and try to remember it. Write out the sentence as many times as you can within two minutes using cursive handwriting.

Animals can be classified into different groups: mammals, birds, reptiles, amphibians, invertebrates and fish.

Self-assessment

Rate your fluency (Could you write smoothly and without effort?) ☆ ☆ ☆

Rate your legibility (Can your writing be easily read by someone else?) ☆ ☆ ☆

Developing a style

Tip!

Handwriting can be adjusted to suit the purpose. When you are taking notes, you might use cursive handwriting to ensure your writing is quick. For labelling maps or filling out forms, you would use print handwriting. If you are creating a presentation or a document for a special occasion, you might add more flourishes to your handwriting.

Trace and then copy the flourished letters below.

a b c d e f g h i j k l m

n o p q r s t u v w x y z

A B C D E F G H I J K L M

N O P Q R S T U V W X Y Z

Write your name and school address using flourished lettering, and then sign off with your personal signature.

Signature: ______________________________

Note-taking

Note-taking is an important skill to learn. Taking notes helps to keep a record of information that you have read or listened to. Sometimes, note-taking may not be very neat, but it should still be legible.

Complete some research on an animal you would like to learn more about. Find out about its appearance, diet, habitat and behaviour.

1. Use the listed websites below to help you research.
2. Write your notes in the box below.

Your note-taking should include the following information.

- Appearance – what does your animal look like?
- Diet – what does it eat?
- Habitat – where does it live?
- Behaviour – how does it move and behave?

Useful sources of information

- Your school library
- https://kids.nationalgeographic.com/animals
- https://animalfactguide.com
- https://www.softschools.com/facts/animals

Consolidating

Start with a compelling introduction that provides a brief overview of your chosen animal and why it's interesting or important. Use your best cursive handwriting, ensuring that your work is neat and legible.

Writing activity

Use your research and your notes to write an engaging and informative text about your chosen animal.

Draw your chosen animal.

Practise your keyboarding skills by typing your text.

Assessment: Legibility

Practise your cursive handwriting as you copy the sentences below.

Many species around the world are facing the threat of extinction due to habitat loss, climate change and other human-related factors. Rainforest species are under enormous threat, mainly due to habitat loss and illegal poaching. Some of the endangered species found in rainforests include orangutans, pygmy elephants, leopards and gorillas. Conservation efforts are crucial to protect these species and preserve the delicate balance of rainforest ecosystems.

Teacher feedback